uman
The Essays

First published in Italy
in 2011 by
Skira Editore S.p.A.
Palazzo Casati Stampa
via Torino 61
20123 Milano
Italy
www.skira.net

Printed and bound in Italy.
First edition

ISBN: 978-88-572-0982-1

Distributed in USA, Canada, Central
& South America by Rizzoli International
Publications, Inc., 300 Park Avenue
South, New York, NY 10010, USA.
Distributed elsewhere in the world
by Thames and Hudson Ltd.,
181A High Holborn, London WC1V 7QX,
United Kingdom.

Nick Foulkes

mogambo
the safari jacket

SKIRA

"In hunting, the finding and killing of game is after all but a part of the whole. The free, self-reliant, adventurous life, with its rugged and stalwart democracy, the wild surroundings, the grand beauty of the scenery, the chance to study the ways and habits of the woodland creatures—all these unite to give to the career of the wilderness hunter its peculiar charm. **The chase is among the best of all national pastimes;** it cultivates that vigorous manliness for the lack of which in a nation, as in an individual, the possession of no other qualities can possibly atone." So wrote one of the great American he-men of the late nineteenth and early twentieth century, Theodore Roosevelt.

And of all the garments in a man's wardrobe, a real man's wardrobe, the safari jacket is arguably the most manly of all;

it speaks to the Hemingway-reading, big game hunter that lurks somewhere within most men. **The architecture of the safari jacket is as familiar as it is practical: four bellows patch pockets with button flaps (or "envelope" pockets as they are referred to by the shirtmakers of London's Jermyn Street). The shirt-like closure at the front finishes with a straight hem at the bottom and a spread collar open at the throat. Button fastened epaulettes can be used to keep binoculars and the like in place. While a cloth belt, in the same fabric, completes its appearance.**

Some years ago I heard that the ultimate safari jacket was made by Abercrombie & Fitch, who at the beginning of the last century, in association with expedition

outfitter Willis & Geiger had developed
a jacket made from a densely woven
cotton (some 240 strands to the inch,
around three times the density of regular
cotton) and given it the romantic name
"model 486". For years I viewed this
jacket as a legend along with the model
476, developed for Papa Hemingway with
a sleeve pocket for his spectacles, and
then one day, while in New York I decided
to pay Abercrombie & Fitch a visit to buy
one... I had arrived too late. The outfitter
who, so legend has it, equipped Roosevelt
for his African soujourn, had become,
as far as I could gather, a nightclub
(albeit one that sold sweatshirts), where
from time to time skimpily-dressed
hard-bodied young models would emerge
from the Stygian gloom. I wonder what
Hemingway and his hero Roosevelt would
have made of that. I returned to London
and promptly did what generations
of Englishmen before me had done and

bespoke a safari suit from my tailor.

After all, it was the British Empire which bequeathed the world the concept of the Safari and its associated paraphernalia. **Africa is the continent with which its association is most enduring and about which the great safari films have been made: *King Solomon's Mines, Mogambo* and of course *Out of Africa.*** The word "safari" is also African in derivation, and it is particularly linked to East Africa, especially what used to be known as British East Africa and is now Kenya, where in Swahili the term refers to a long journey, which in turn is derived from the Arabic "safar" (meaning journey, trip, or tour). And in 1902, when the King's African Rifles was raised in the various African territories controlled by Britain,

1 *The Man Eaters of Tsavo and other East African Adventures.* p. 27.

its Regimental March was the oddly contradictory "Funga Safari" (Halt the March), a jaunty number so beloved of the service that it was adopted on independence by the Kenya Rifles.

Although the term entered the English language in the latter half of the nineteenth century, it was still enough of a neologism at the beginning of the twentieth century for author, engineer and hunter Colonel John Henry Patterson, DSO to have to explain it in parentheses describing it as a "caravan journey" in his classic 1907 account of lion-hunting: *The Man Eaters of Tsavo and other East African Adventures.*[1] The Colonel, something of a hero to Roosevelt by the way, was despatched to British East Africa to superintend the building of a railway. But on arrival he had to track and kill two lions that had eaten dozens of construction workers. *The Man Eaters of Tsavo* was twice made into a film: once as a 3D shocker called *Bwana Devil* (strap line: The Miracle of the Age!!! A LION in your lap! A LOVER in your arms!); and then again in the 1990s as *The Ghost and the Darkness* starring Michael Douglas and Val Kilmer.

However, it was not in Africa, but in India that the concept of the safari and the safari jacket was born; the East India Company was able to trace its foundation back to the end of the sixteenth century, and when not involved in subduing the native inhabitants and extending the orbit of British influence, the young men of the British East India Company sought risk and adventure in the hunting of the big game. Tigers and elephants topped the list of trophies while the principles of fox hunting were adapted

2 Quoted by Major-General J. G. Elliott in *Field Sports in India 1800–1947*, pp. 22–23.

to pigsticking, whereby wild boar were chased on horseback and killed using a long spear. At a time of inaccurate, muzzle loading, low velocity guns (the flintlock smoothbore musket remained standard issue in the British military long into the nineteenth century), the game hunters had to get close to their quarry: one towering figure of the British India, General John Nicholson's preferred mode of tiger hunting was to ride round them until they became dizzy, at which point he would finish them off at close quarters with cold steel.

Life on those early hunting adventures was exhilarating and dangerous but it was also luxurious; in his memoir *War and Sport in India*, Lieutenant John Pester recounts how, when not fighting the Mahrattas, he would venture forth with "guns, elephants, servants with

a good store of claret, Madeira fowls, hams, etc."[2] to bag himself some trophies.
And it was in India that the image of the big game hunter began to be formed and it was here that the safari jacket began to evolve. In his book *Seonee, or Camp Life on the Satpura Range*, Sir Robert Armitage Sterndale records the appearance of the archetypal big game hunter of the subcontinent. The Shikaris (from the Sanskrit for hunter or guide) of nineteenth-century India were the forerunners of the great white hunters of twentieth-century Africa.

"Clad in a close fitting suit of stout drill, dyed with the barks of the mango and babool trees to the true shikar colour; the shoulders protected by pieces of leather to bear the friction of the rifle; leather-lined

3 *Seonee, or Camp Life on the Satpura Range,* 1877, p. 10.

4 Leatrice Eiseman, *The Color Answer Book from the World's Leading Color Expert,* p. 53.

pockets in front to hold a small powder flask, caps, and a ball, sewed up in a greased cloth; a kookri or Gurkha knife and a short-bladed, straight, double-edged dagger attached to a broad belt of sambhur leather; leggings of the same material completed his attire."[3]

Architecture aside, colour, as described above, is the other key identifier of the safari jacket. **It is usually executed in varying shades from sage to sand, which come under the umbrella term khaki and once again it is from India, in particular the Punjab that the term (from the Urdu word for dust-coloured) and the colour originate.** The man responsible for introducing the now ubiquitous colour to the British military was

Lieutenant-General Sir Harry Burnett
Lumsden. A true old India hand,
Lumsden was born aboard an East India
vessel in the Bay of Bengal and, becoming
a soldier in his teens, he was involved
in opening the Khyber Pass in 1842
and raised a special forces unit called
the Corps of Guides five years later.
Intended for work on reconnaissance
and intelligence gathering missions,
the unit was characterized by an
unorthodox approach to uniforms.
Lumsden eschewed the traditional red
coats of the British military, feeling
better able to fight in the pyjama-style
local dress that had been dyed the colour
of mud, using a dye that came from
a plant called Mazari.

According to one source "the regiment
was renamed the *mudlarks*",[4] but the
ribaldry soon gave way to an appreciation
of the practicality and comfort of khaki,

1 *The chicest interpretation
of a safari jacket by Lord
Curzon, the Viceroy of India.
Here with his wife and
an "impressive prey"*

2 *Clark Gable, the unforgettable
character of the movie*
Mogambo, *1953*

3 *Yves Saint Laurent and
two of his muses, Betty Catroux,
modelling his famous safari
outfit, and Louise de La Falaise
in front of the YSL boutique
in London, 1969*

4 *Stephen Mills,*
The History of Muthaiga
Country Club
*Bookcover of Volume I,
1913–1963*

George Hugh Stutchbury
Muthaiga's first Club
Secretary - 1914

5 Major-General
J. G. Elliott, *Field Sports
in India 1800–1947*,
p. 23.

and the cloth was adopted piecemeal by units of the British Army engaged in colonial wars under the fierce sun of the tropics and the equator. However, it was not until 1884 that khaki was officially adopted by the British Army. In part this must have been due to the fact that a colourfast khaki dye was only patented that year and hitherto the desired hue had been achieved, with varying degrees of success, using such colorants as macerated tobacco juice, coffee and tea. Moreover, the introduction of khaki as an official uniform must, in some part, have been hastened by the humiliating defeat of the British redcoats at Iswalanda during the Anglo–Zulu war of 1879.

It was also about this time that the first game laws began to be introduced in India. Up until the end of the 1870s the great Shikaris had been able to treat the entirety of British India as one great

hunting ground and, unfettered by much
in the way of limits on the numbers and
species of animals they shot, they had
killed at will. "In fact it was a matter
of government policy to clear whole
areas of game to open up fresh tracts for
cultivation."[5] But in the 1880s, the tide
began to turn towards conservation and
the hunters (many of them from India)
turned their attention to the big game
of Africa.

One of the first Britons to hunt in Africa
was Major Sir William Cornwallis Harris,
an engineer in the Indian Army who was
drawn to the Transvaal by the accounts
of the abundant game in Zululand given
by an early explorer. Accompanied by
a friend from the Bombay Civil Service
he set off with sixteen oxen and
a wagon laden with six months supplies
and 18,000 lead bullets along with
further ingots of lead and bullet moulds

6 Dennis Holman,
Inside Safari Hunting,
p. 11.

should they run out. They were not disappointed: in one day alone they were obliged to kill four white rhino... just in self-defence. And their favoured method of downing a giraffe, or cameleopard as it was picturesquely known, was to ride alongside, shoot it and then leap on its back and ride it until it fell. They came away with "two perfect heads of every species of quadruped to be found in southern Africa, together with skins of lions, leopards, ostriches, crocodiles, the tusks of elephants and hippopotami, the horns of rhinoceros, besides drawings of every animal of interest to the sportsman".[6]

Harris wrote a stirring account of the trip called *The Wild Sports of Southern Africa*, which in the words of safari historian Dennis Holman, "can be said to have started what was to become the most prestigious pastime of the gentleman".

But these gentlemen had to be intrepid and rich: whereas in India field sports were open to even junior officers, Africa remained terra incognita. "Few were prepared to brave the perils of a journey into the unknown and fewer still could afford it." But then in the 1880s British East Africa opened up, with the Empire establishing Somaliland as a protectorate and founding the Imperial British East Africa Company in 1888 to develop the huge territory that corresponds today to Kenya and Uganda; railways began to cut into the virgin land and ever bigger steamships docked in Mombassa.

The safari began to boom.

It was the time of giants like Cecil Rhodes and the quasi-mythical legendary hunter Frederick Courtenay Selous, who is said to have inspired Sir Henry Rider Haggard's *Allan Quatermain*.

7 Dennis Holman, *Inside Safari Hunting*, p. 39.

These were the days of big men with big guns: one of them, Sir Samuel Baker, went after elephants with a behemoth of a rifle made for him by Holland & Holland and that fired an exploding shell into the oncoming pachyderm. It never failed to kill, but it was almost as hazardous for the hunter as his quarry: "this instrument of torture to the hunter was not sufficiently heavy for the weight of the projectile: it only weighted twenty pounds, thus with a charge of ten drachms of powder and a HALF-POUND shell, the recoil was so terrific, that I spun around like a weathercock in a hurricane".

Nairobi quickly became the big game hunting headquarters of the world; between 1902 and 1906 it tripled in size and in the space of three or four years its cemetery filled up with over fifty white hunters.

On paying it a visit Theodore Roosevelt was struck with the number of tombstones bearing the same epitaph, "Killed by a Lion".[7]

By now the khaki safari jacket had emerged in the form we know it today, indeed khaki had been adopted by many of the world's armed forces; including those of America. Roosevelt had worn a khaki tunic very similar to a safari jacket as commander of the Rough Riders in the Spanish–American War.

The explorer and colonial administrator Sir Frederick Jackson recommended clothes of "Kharki [sic] and Indian shikar cloth" cut in the style of a Norfolk jacket with pockets "fairly large and roomy" covered by a "good deep flap" fastened with a button.

Sir Frederick also preferred a single

8 Quoted by Kenneth Cameron, *Into Africa*, p. 120.

outbreast pocket on the left, but nothing on the right so that there would be nothing for the butt of his gun to snag on when mounting a rifle to take a shot. He also specified two rows of cartridge loops "for the cartridges of the two Express rifles most in use".[8]

The Boer War at the beginning of the nineteenth century had a marked influence on the development of the safari suit. Burberry, which had outfitted many of the British officers, segued effortlessly into the peacetime needs of the big game hunter, advertising the gabardine suit, the illustration showing a man in a slouch hat, rifle broken over one arm, a cartridge belt around his waist and a native bearer and tent in the background.

The safari jacket was taken very seriously as a functional and

protective garment, thus along with its voluminous pockets and cartridge loops, it often came with an additional spine pad that buttoned onto the back of the jacket. In the Guards Museum in London there is an example of a khaki military tunic from the Sudan War complete with this cumbersome addition; at the time it was thought that sunstroke was contracted by exposure of the spine to the sun.

Before and immediately after the Second World War a sense of glamour attached itself to the safari jacket. This was the era of the Happy Valley crowd, hedonistic adulterers frittering away their lives in a champagne haze of sex and

9 Winston Churchill writing in *The New York Times*, 2 May 1909.

shooting—at least that was the popular impression. And the safari was the ultimate leisure activity for English aristocrats, Indian princelings, American industrialists and Hollywood movie stars.

But it was also the time of ever more vocal aspirations to independence and here again the safari suit had its part to play. Before the First World War, Churchill had already noticed the habit among African chiefs of dressing in Western clothes, khaki safari jackets, pith helmets and the like. He had been unimpressed. "The chiefs", he wrote in May 1909, "succeed in reducing themselves to regular guys.
Any old cast-off khaki jacket or tattered pair of trousers; any fragment of weather-stained uniform, a battered sun helmet with a feather stuck lamely into

the top of it, a ragged umbrella,
is sufficient to induce them to abandon
the ostrich plume and the leopard
skin Kaross. Among their warriors in
ancient gear they look ridiculous and
insignificant—more like the commonest
kind of native sweeper than the
hereditary rulers of the powerful and
numerous tribes."[9]
The British saw a fierce and noble
pageantry in traditional African dress;
as Captain J. D. Falcon, a British
officer touring Nigeria in 1910, wrote
of a gathering of an emir's court with
all its courtiers in cloaks of many
colours and attendant slaves, guards
and horsemen: **"It was a scene
of barbaric splendor, a page
from a medieval romance, and
behind came the incongruous
khaki-clad Briton, with his
twentieth-century equipment
carried by porters for whom**

26

10 Quoted in
*Fashioning Africa:
Power and the Politics
of Dress*, p. 129.

11 *Fashioning Africa:
Power and the Politics
of Dress*, p. 169.

it was difficult to find a setting in either the old or new regime".[10] This was a patronising view that took what amounted to an amused ethnographical interest in what colonial expatriates saw as little more than charming local customs, a sort of historical pantomime that was amusing as a tourist attraction.

However, by the time Harold Macmillan made his famous "wind of change" speech in South Africa in 1960, signalling that Britain was ready to grant independence to its African colonies with the line, "The wind of change is blowing through this continent. Whether we like it or not, this growth of national consciousness is a political fact", both the departing colonialists and the incoming nationalists adopted variations on the quasi-military safari suit. Having been patronised for years when wearing national dress, the safari suit, the ubiquitous dress of

27

the outgoing caste of white civil servants and administrators, was seen as the default garment of the governing class, whether British or indigenous. At least in the early days of independence of some countries, cultural nationalism as expressed through dress was played down in favour of the perceived seriousness of the Western safari suit. The lasting sartorial legacy of Kenneth Kaunda, the first president of independent Zambia, is the popularisation of the safari suit; so associated is he with it that "in the neighbouring countries, 'Kaunda' has become a term of the bush suit of colonial vintage that he popularised as the 'safari suit' in Zambia".[11]

Indeed the national coat-of-arms of Zambia features a man dressed in a short sleeved safari suit, better to demonstrate the dynamic modernity and intrinsic capacity for self-government of the newly born nation.

According to one who was a young army officer at the time, "as the colonies began to break away there was increasing self-consciousness about the colonial behaviour. Kenya became independent in 1963, and Kenyatta (Mzee Jomo, 'The Old Man') was brought in out of the cold from prison in Mauritius. Ironically he often wore a Safari Suit, as did many of the new native Caribbean Governors—it took some time before they wore their native dress and they often dressed more in a colonial style than their predecessors."

And it was perhaps this sudden proliferation of the safari suit in its new guise as the uniform of emancipation across the tropics that brought it to the attention of French designers Yves Saint Laurent and Ted Lapidus. By 1968 the wind of change was blowing along the boulevards and gusting down the avenues of the French capital as established order seemed to break down in the face of student anarchy. The wind of change also whistled down the catwalk that year as Yves Saint Laurent gave his take on the safari suit, the lace-fronted Saharienne, which also gave the fashion of the swinging decade what is arguably its most sexy image, the model Verushka in sultry pose, a rifle across her shoulders and plenty of flesh visible beneath the lacing.

Meanwhile flesh of a less attractive kind was on display under the safari suit in another of Britain's former colonies. It had no big game hunting tradition to speak of, although kangaroo shooting is a popular recreation, nevertheless **the safari suit played an important part in Australian life during the 1970s, when for a time it was deemed acceptable**

30

12 BBC website,
Friday, 5 December
2003.

in politics and business.

Among the parliamentarians seen in the
safari suit was John Howard; and outside
the stock exchange in Adelaide there used
to be a notice which read "Members NOT
wearing a safari suit require a jacket and
tie". It was perhaps the adoption by the
political and business elite of Australia as
well as its tongue-in-cheek espousal by
Roger Moore's James Bond that accounted
for the garment's declining popularity
during the 1980s and 1990s.

**However, rather like the
Shikars of the Raj and
the hunters of colonial Africa,
the safari suit is made of
stern stuff. It will take more
than a decline in big game
hunting; a post colonial
backlash; and the attentions
of Australian businessmen
to polish off the safari suit.**

Even now in the twenty-first century it continues to be associated with the brave and pioneering spirit that built the British Empire. In 2003, the British Broadcasting Corporation conducted some research into its public perception. It was particularly keen to know what viewers and listeners thought of the BBC in the Britain of Tony Blair's New Labour, a classless country characterized by an overwhelming political correctness. Reassuringly or irritatingly, depending on your point of view, the BBC's use of the term "correspondent" conjured up a particularly vivid picture of "intrepid reporters with upper-class accents and... what else... safari suits".[12]

François Berthoud
Born in Switzerland,
1961, lives and works in
Zurich. He is known for
his fashion illustrations.
Since the mid-1980s,
François Berthoud has
been mainly engaged
in artistic activities.
His high-impact images
bring art, fashion
and communication
together. He has
published books, staged
exhibitions and realized
special fashion projects.
He is a contributor
to major magazines
worldwide.

Nick Foulkes is the
critically acclaimed
author of Dancing
Into Battle: A Social
History of the Battle
of Waterloo and
at least a dozen other
books on subjects as
diverse as the history
of the Trench coat
and American high
society. In 2007 he
was named Havana
Man of the Year. In
Debrett's his leisure
interests are listed as
playing backgammon
and visiting watch
and cigar factories.